ABYSSINIANS

MARYSA STORM

BLACK
RABBIT
BOOKS

Bolt Jr. is published by Black Rabbit Books
P.O. Box 227, Mankato, Minnesota, 56002.
www.blackrabbitbooks.com
Copyright © 2025 Black Rabbit Books

Alissa Thielges, editor
Rhea Magaro, designer

Names: Storm, Marysa, author.
Title: Abyssinians / by Marysa Storm.
Description: Mankato, MN : Black Rabbit Books, [2025] |
 Series: Bolt Jr.
Our favorite cats | Includes bibliographical references
 and index. | Audience: Ages 5-8 | Audience: Grades
 K-1 | Summary: "Beginning readers will fall in love with
 Abyssinian cats as they explore the breed's unique features,
 playful personality, and pet care through closely leveled
 text, engaging designs, and playful, vibrant photography"--
 Provided by publisher.
Identifiers: LCCN 2024010399 (print) | LCCN 2024010400
 (ebook) | ISBN 9781644666760 (library binding) | ISBN
 9781644666944 (ebook)
Subjects: LCSH: Abyssinian cat--Juvenile literature.
Classification: LCC SF449.A28 S767 2025 (print) | LCC
 SF449.A28 (ebook) | DDC 636.8/26--dc23/eng/20240425
LC record available at https://lccn.loc.gov/2024010399
LC ebook record available at https://lccn.loc.
 gov/2024010400

Image Credits

Dreamstime/Natalya Gavrilova, 20–21; Getty/Betsey Leavitt
Josselyn, 5; Shutterstock/Alla Lla, 1, Anastasia Vetkovskaya, 12,
Andrew Shevchuk, 19, Dr.Margorius, 8–9, Eric Isselee, 7, 21,
Kasefoto, 13, Kyselova Inna, cover, marinaks, 23, maritime_m, 14,
Nan Liu, 18, nelik, 4, Oksana Bystritskaya, 11, Polina Tomtosova, 3,
24, Roman Zaiets, 17, Roxana Bashyrova, 10, WildStrawberry, 6

Contents

Chapter 1
Meet the Abyssinian .. 4

Chapter 2
Personality 10

Chapter 3
Abyssinian Care 16

More Information 22

Meet the Abyssinian

A tan cat gazes at a shelf. It's the perfect spot. Its strong **limbs** hop onto the sofa. Then it leaps up to the bookshelf. The cat relaxes. It loves to climb to high places.

limb: a leg or an arm

COMPARING SIZES

Abyssinian ◀ ⋯⋯⋯
8 to 12 pounds
(4 to 5.5 kg)

Strong Cats

Abyssinians love to climb. Their powerful legs help them leap. They have long bodies and tails, small paws, and big ears. Their coats are often gray, reddish, or light brown.

. . . ▶ **Maine Coon**
8 to 18 pounds
(4 to 8 kg)

PARTS OF AN
Abyssinian

lean body

long tail

almond-
shaped
eyes

big
ears

small
paws

9

CHAPTER 2

Personality

Abyssinians are playful and smart. They can learn to play fetch. These cats like to **investigate**. Sometimes they run off with things they shouldn't.

investigate: to find out information about something

FACT

They are called Abys for short.

Friendly Cats

These cats love **company**. They like to be around their owners. They will even make friends with other animals. They will cuddle up with other cats and nice dogs.

company: being with another person

Where Abyssinians Came From

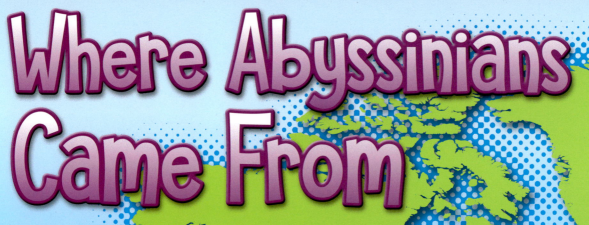

People think Abys came from an area now called Egypt.

North America

Egypt

CHAPTER 3

Abyssinian Care

Abys need care. Their teeth need to be cleaned. Their nails should be trimmed. Their short coats don't need a lot of brushing. But they need more brushing when they shed.

FACT

Cats shed in the spring and fall.

Curious Cats

Vet visits are important too. Vets keep pets healthy. Abys are curious cats. They love to explore. Some may even like going outside. They need love and plenty of toys.

Abyssinians' Height
**12 to 16 inches
(30.5 to 40.5 centimeters)**

Bonus Facts

Their eyes are usually green or gold.

Abys live up to **15 years.**

They can jump up to 6 feet (2 meters) high.

Their coat is **ticked.**

ticked: bands of color on a strand of hair that are darker at the tip

21

READ MORE/WEBSITES

Burling, Alexis. *Cats.* Minneapolis: Abdo Publishing Company, 2024.

Wilson, Sierra. *Abyssinian.* Fantastic Cats. New York: Lightbox Learning, 2024.

Woodson, Cameron L. *Abyssinians.* Cat Club. Minneapolis: Jump!, 2021.

Abyssinian
kids.britannica.com/students/article/ Abyssinian/309663

Abyssinian Cat Breed
cats.com/cat-breeds/abyssinian

Cats Rule in Ancient Egypt
kids.nationalgeographic.com/pages/article/ cats-rule-in-ancient-egypt

GLOSSARY

company (KUHM -puh-nee)—being with another person

investigate (in-VES-tuh-gayt)—to find out information about something

limb (LYM)—a leg or an arm

ticked (TIKT)—bands of color on a stand of hair that are darker at the tip

INDEX

B

body parts, 4, 7, 8–9, 20
breed origin, 14–15

C

care, 16, 21
coats, 7, 16, 21

L

life spans, 20

P

personality, 4, 7, 10, 13, 19

S

size, 6, 19